The Life Balance Hacks Series: Hack #1

Time Concentration

More LIFE in the Time You Have

Daniel Gentry

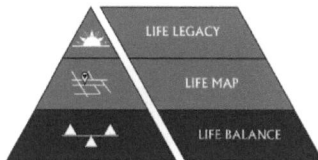

The Life Triad - Foundation

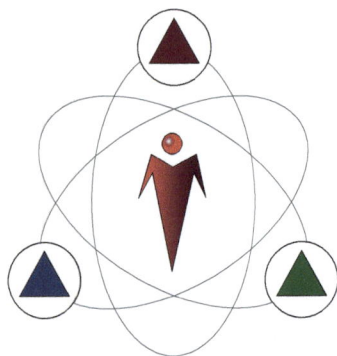

Third Power
Performance

405 SE Osceola Ave. # 104
Ocala, FL 34471

(352) 462-4518

www.ThirdPowerPerformance.com

ISBN-13: 978-0-9977846-4-0

The reason this book exists:

My wife that gives me love, support, and insights when I lack inspiration.

My son Anthony who gives me silly the looks that warm my heart and remind me to keep my inner child alive.

My son Daniel who is becoming a man before my eyes. Don't be in too much of a hurry to grow up.

My daughters, Anisa, Victoria, and Elizabeth, I am so proud of the fine women you have become. I am prouder of you than you can imagine.

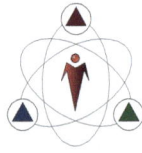

INTRODUCTION

RAINBOWS AND

SKITTLES

I had my epiphany many years ago when I realized I was working myself to death. I was making good money and was successful in my career, but the rest of my life was in shambles. Shortly after that my life did fall apart completely. I lost everything. I was divorced, jobless, and broke. As I struggled to rebuild my life, I resolved I would not let that happen again, and if I could help it, to anyone else either.

In my quest to find a way to not only have life balanced but true success and fulfillment, I created my Life Triad system. A complete system for Life Balance, creating a Life Map (goals) and building a real Life Legacy.

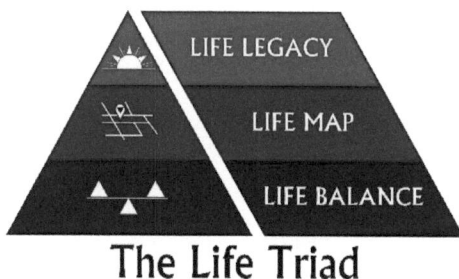

LIFE LEGACY

LIFE MAP

LIFE BALANCE

The Life Triad

Once, during a seminar, I had just completed the life balance portion of my program. I had talked all about the different aspects of life balance, the self-mastery, the relationships, the material prosperity, and showed how you must have a plan for being balanced and how it will always be a work in progress. We were having questions and answers afterwards and one of the participants says:

> *"You know what, enough with the rainbows and Skittles, okay? This all sounds great, but there are days when I have deadlines. There are things that have to get done, fires come up, I'm workin' the weekend. How does this help with that?"*

And so, I wanted to address the "rainbows and Skittles" aspect. So often, the idea of life balance is very nice, and it's soft and squishy. Let's talk about how you apply it in the real world? In this eBook I would like to share with you one of my most powerful tools for actually enabling life balance. I call it...

Time Concentration.

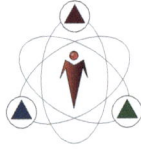

CHAPTER 1

TIME

CONCENTRATION

We all have busy lives. We know life balance is important, but how do we accomplish all that we need to do in our careers and still have an amazing and fulfilling life? In my live programs, we spend a lot of time working on finding your purpose and building out your Life Legacy design. This "ultimate destination" allows us to make better day to day decisions about the tasks we focus upon. It also allows us to rethink what we are already doing with the filter of how to get the most out of those moments.

The basic idea of time concentration is not so much about adding tasks to our day, but in concentrating the life we put into those tasks. One key to achieving life balance is doing multiple things simultaneously!

I can hear the objections already. Multitasking is bad. It has been proven repeatedly that as humans, we cannot really do multitasking. We can't do two activities simultaneously. We just switch between things quickly and lose efficiency. Right.

Not multitasking, Time Concentration!

The idea can be summed up in one sentence:

Take multiple parts of life and combine it into one activity.

This may sound simple, but it is powerful! We can choose an activity we are hyper-focused on which will actually enhance multiple areas of life balance. It requires us to be fully in the moment. A walk to the car from the grocery store can be spiritually enlightening if we take the time to notice the rainbow everyone else is too busy to see. The trip up one floor to a colleague's office can be a moment to increase our health if we focus and take the stairs.

The key is being intentional with our activities and keeping them always focused on our life's purpose.

This is not to say you are not allowed to have downtime. There is a huge benefit and need for doing "nothing" and letting the mind rest. However, in our world today, the real threat we face is having so much to do that requires no real thought. We have all had the experience of sitting down to check email or social media and suddenly an hour is just gone (or maybe four).

Recipe for blackened chicken: 1 - Put chicken in oven. 2 - Go quickly check your Facebook feed.

The best way to explain Time Concentration is to show you how it works. I've compiled a list of five time concentration examples for you to use right now. But this just scratches the surface.

Before we get into the examples, I wanted to touch quickly on how I define Life Balance.

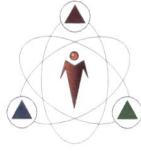

CHAPTER 2

DEFINING LIFE

BALANCE

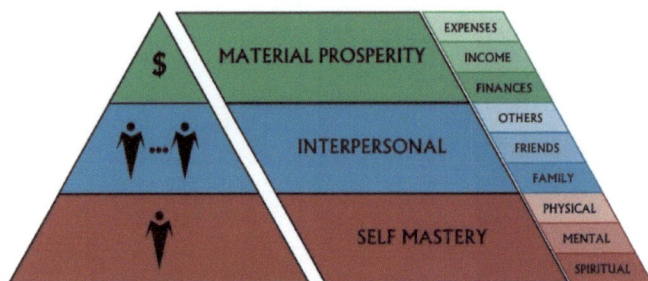

The Life Balance Triad

The concept of life balance in this eBook is based on my Life Balance Triad. This is the foundation of my life transformational program. The Life Balance Triad concept breaks life balance into three parts: self-mastery, interpersonal (our relationships), and material prosperity. Each of those breaks down into three subsequent pieces.

- ⅄ Self-mastery
  - o Spiritual - Our philosophical and spiritual foundation
  - o Mental - The framework of our knowledge and emotions

- Physical - The manifestation of our being

▲ Interpersonal
- Family - Foundation of all our relationships
- Friends - Our network and the framework of our relationships
- Others - How do we make a difference in the world - people we don't know.

▲ Material prosperity
- Finances - Our Financial Foundation: financial education, budget, investment plan, etc.
- Income - How we make money
- Expenses - What we buy with our money, our "stuff"

As we go through the examples in this book, the areas of life balance affected will be highlighted with the following graphic:

SELF MASTERY			INTERPERSONAL			MATERIAL PROSPERITY		
SPIRITUAL	MENTAL	PHYSICAL	FAMILY	FRIENDS	OTHERS	FINANCES	INCOME	EXPENSES

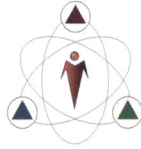

CHAPTER 3

EXAMPLE #1

CHOOSE A FITNESS PROGRAM TO MAXIMIZE YOUR LIFE

SELF MASTERY			INTERPERSONAL			MATERIAL PROSPERITY		
SPIRITUAL	MENTAL	PHYSICAL	FAMILY	FRIENDS	OTHERS	FINANCES	INCOME	EXPENSES

We have many choices when choosing how we want to get the exercise our body desperately needs. Do we join a gym? Do we do CrossFit? Yoga? Pilates? There are so many choices.

I will not tell you what to choose. What I will say is choose an exercise that will allow a greater experience of life.

There are endless ways to enhance your exercise routine that can create a more fulfilling life, and if you don't have a solid routine yet, now is the time to choose something that will boost your life balance!

⋏ Find something the whole family can enjoy that will bring you closer and gives you a common experience to talk about.

⋏ Alter activities so they tap into your spiritual experiences. Instead of just walking on a treadmill, find a beautiful park to walk in. Listen to something uplifting while you exercise.

⅄ Expand your mind. Find workouts that require concentration or listen to educational audios during your workout.

⅄ Consider the peer group you would like to be around personally and professionally. What do they do for fitness?

My Life Example

I do karate as my exercise of choice, and I do it with my entire family. This allows me several benefits. It's a very good exercise. I'm going three to four times a week. So physically, it's very good for me. Karate also has a strong mental component because you need full concentration and you're learning the moves. It requires your mind. You really have to be there. It's not just like running or something where you can just kind of do it mindlessly. You really have to focus and pay attention so it brings in the mental aspect of ourselves very much.

For me personally, I actually find a spiritual aspect of it too--the concentration, the quieting of the mind, and the breathing. There's a magic to the movements of it that touches on the spiritual.

Since I do it with my family, my boys and I have stuff to talk about. We're working on the same forms, and we have shared experiences that we can really talk about over the dinner table. If you have younger children, sometimes it can be a challenge to know the latest cool thing, right? So, this gives us a common thread to be able to really talk.

I've made new friends, plus I have friends I found out were going there as well so it has strengthened those friendships. In addition, I have actually made business connections through the adults at classes (both parents of kids in the class and adults in the class). So, it's helped my financial life.

This one activity that I'm very involved in and very hyper-focused on actually pulls in six aspects of life balance. It's concentrating that time and maximizing the amount of life in that hour or two each time I go. It's an amazing, amazing thing.

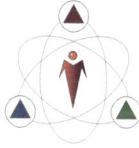

CHAPTER 4

EXAMPLE #2

COMBINE WORK AND EXERCISE

SELF MASTERY			INTERPERSONAL			MATERIAL PROSPERITY		
SPIRITUAL	MENTAL	**PHYSICAL**	FAMILY	FRIENDS	OTHERS	FINANCES	**INCOME**	EXPENSES

The reality of life is that we spend much of our days working, and it's difficult to find time for as much physical activity as we need. While this will not replace your normal workouts, it makes a difference, doctors say any amount of exercise helps -- the benefits are cumulative. This can also be a major stress reliever and reduce burnout. Some can be done while you work, others during breaks (see Chapter 5).

Working while you exercise can be done by getting a hands-free phone headset and walking while on the phone, or by getting a desk cycle (do a quick search on Amazon for "desk cycle" for many options).

Make the most of your breaks. Here are just a few of my favorites that are easy to add to any break:

Quick Exercises

- ▲ Do a football-like drill of running in place for 60 seconds. Get those knees up! (If just starting, march in place.)

- ▲ Do walk-lunges in your office or a vacant room (or if you are ok with looking odd, do it in open spaces).

- ▲ Sitting leg lifts: Sitting in your chair, lift one leg off the seat, extend it out straight, hold for 2 seconds; then lower your foot (but don't put it on the floor) and hold for several seconds. Switch; do each leg 15 times.

Quick Stretches

- ▲ Sitting tall in your chair, stretch both arms over your head and reach upward. After about 10 seconds, extend the right hand higher, then the left.

- Sitting up straight, try to touch your shoulder blades together. Hold, and then relax.

- To relieve tension, try this yoga posture: Sit facing forward, then turn your head to the left and your torso to the right, and hold a few seconds. If you are in a swivel chair, do not be tempted to turn the chair. Repeat 10-15 times, alternating sides.

My Life Example

I spend large amounts of time on the phone--conference calls, meeting with clients, sales calls. I bought a nice Bluetooth headset like what you would see in a call center. The microphone has noise canceling and lots of other features. I actually go on walks around my neighborhood while I'm making my calls. So, I'm out getting fresh air and seeing different scenery rather than the poster on the wall that I've seen 100 million times. I'm actually less distracted than when I'm sitting in front of my computer because there is always that tendency to look at email or calendar to see what's coming up next. There are all these distractions, and oddly enough, it's less distracting being outside.

I'm getting physical exercise. I'm not walking vigorously but just walking around getting fresh air, and when I have one of those calls... you know the one, the really annoying phone call or the phone call that challenges us, right? Well, I'm able to take a minute after that call, breathe, look around, and look at the nice blue sky. Then I gather myself back before I move on to my next call. It's a huge stress reliever.

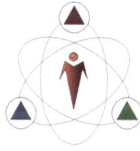

CHAPTER 5

EXAMPLE #3

POMODORO
TECHNIQUE
"PLUS"

SELF MASTERY			INTERPERSONAL			MATERIAL PROSPERITY		
SPIRITUAL	MENTAL	PHYSICAL	FAMILY	FRIENDS	OTHERS	FINANCES	INCOME	EXPENSES

Now that you have some good ideas for exercise during breaks, when should you take a break?

Use the Pomodoro Technique!

If you're not familiar with the Pomodoro Technique, this is a time management strategy that is very common among software developers. You pick a single task, work on it for 25 minutes with real focus, and then take a five-minute break. After four "Pomodoros" take a longer break of 15 – 30 minutes. There are many apps available for phones, computers, and more. Just search for "Pomodoro", and you will find a number of them.

Shut off all email, alerts, phone ringer, anything that will interrupt you. I used to put up a sign outside my cube to let people know I was on a focused task and not to interrupt me for anything trivial.

You want to be focused and concentrating for that 25 minutes.

What makes it the Pomodoro Technique "PLUS" is what you do during your break. Take some exercises and stretches from Chapter 4 and use them frequently. However, those are not the only things to plug in to build life balance.

Five-Minute Break Ideas:

⅄ Three-minute gratitude session. Take just a few minutes to be thankful for all you have.

⅄ Step outside and call your mom, dad, grandparent, sibling, or other family member just to say hi and see how the day is going. They will appreciate it and you will feel good too.

⅄ Have a quick meditation session.

⅄ Refill your water to stay hydrated.

- ⅄ Send a thank you note to someone who's helped you out recently—your assistant who's gone above and beyond or a co-worker who proofread a report for you.

- ⅄ Unsubscribe from newsletters in your inbox. That travel deals newsletter you haven't actually read in months? Get it out of there. The email list you never signed up for but somehow got on anyway? Gone. Anything you haven't read in a month or more? You probably don't need to be getting it every day.

15 to 30-Minute Break Ideas:

- ⅄ Take a quick 15 to 20-minute nap (if you have somewhere private and safe). You will be amazed at the difference it will make with how you feel.

- Find inspiring stories to read to motivate and excite you. TED Talks are a great place to start or just check out ThirdPowerPerformance.com for the latest blog post.

- Keep a non-work book to read on these breaks. It will feel good to not stare at a computer screen for a while, and a great book can be inspiring.

My Life Example

This technique is something that I use every day. I'm in a pomodoro right now. I am in minute 12 with another 13 minutes before my next 30 minute break and I will be taking a nap. This has been huge for my productivity by itself. Add in the life balance boosting breaks and it brought my life to a new level. Plus, I **LOVE** naps!

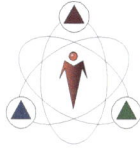

CHAPTER 6

EXAMPLE #4

THROW AN INVENTORY OR CLEAN-UP PARTY

SELF MASTERY			INTERPERSONAL			MATERIAL PROSPERITY		
SPIRITUAL	MENTAL	PHYSICAL	FAMILY	FRIENDS	OTHERS	FINANCES	INCOME	EXPENSES

In my training programs, I talk about how the biggest hidden thief of life balance is our possessions. Everything you own also owns you! Think about it. Do you have a car? You must fill it with gas, change the oil, wash it, store it, worry about where you park it, change tires, etc. Golf clubs, or other sporting equipment? Store it, clean it, organize it, etc. Everything you own takes energy, time and money. How many of us have a garage full of stuff? Closets? Drawers? Storage units?

Time to clean house, figuratively and literally, with a clean-up/inventory party. Find an area accumulating a lot of junk. Sometimes it's just that drawer in the kitchen we all have or maybe it's something larger like a big closet or the garage or even a whole room. For smaller jobs, just get your immediate family together, or for those big jobs, like the garage, I invite over extended family and friends I can trust and we get to work on cleaning out all the stuff that's in the offending area.

As you are organizing, you need to do an inventory of how much stuff do you actually have. Ask yourself, are these things serving my greater good? Do they help me achieve my Life Legacy? For everything not serving you and helping you achieve your goals, give them away. This is a way to serve your community and help others that are less fortunate than you. Many services will actually come and pick up stuff from your house to give to charity. Plus, there are even tax incentives to donating things you don't need to charity.

Then you buy pizza, grill burgers and hotdogs, or whatever works for you and have a party! **Make it fun!**

Our garage was full of junk, Boy Scout stuff and all kinds of things that I needed to clean or get rid of. I invited over my niece and some friends and together with my wife and boys we went through it and got it all cleaned out.

I donated a ton of things to charity and wrote off several hundreds of dollars on my taxes.

Now we can actually walk through the garage! The best part was throwing a party and having a blast with family and friends.

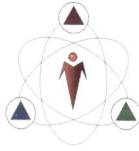

CHAPTER 7

EXAMPLE #5

CREATE AWESOME FAMILY TIME

SELF MASTERY			INTERPERSONAL			MATERIAL PROSPERITY		
SPIRITUAL	MENTAL	PHYSICAL	FAMILY	FRIENDS	OTHERS	FINANCES	INCOME	EXPENSES

For many of us, family time is often one of the most difficult things to plan, and yet one of the things that we wish we had more of. I've compiled a small list of things we can do together as a family to bring everyone together to not only be together but to improve everyone's lives.

Story Time

A way to bring the family together is by reading good books and hearing good stories. This is especially great for inviting parents, grandparents, aunts, uncles, etc., and creating that familial bond, not just in your core unit but also expanding out to your extended family ties. Plus, it's a lot of fun. You get people together, and tell stories about your childhood, about the past, and your family history. It's really a very cool way to pull people together.

Family Reading Time

Read a book together. Some of my best memories were my stepfather reading Sherlock Homes stories on the two-hour drive to Tampa. It made me appreciate literature and created a very strong bond in our family. Take the time to read with your family and to your children, the memories that they will have will last forever.

Or, you can do a family book report (for the kids, I wouldn't call it a book report) where everybody reads something that they find interesting and then shares it all together. You're increasing your knowledge, and you're also increasing family cohesion.

Create a Menu for the Week

Have you ever heard the question "what should we have for dinner?" If it has been asked once, it's been asked a million times. The solution? Have a meal planning session.

Create a master list of dishes that are popular, then you can choose which dishes you want to have each day plus list out when you want to eat out.

Create a grid for the days of the week and take meals from your master list to put on each day. In my programs, I have worksheets that make this fairly straightforward if you would like a copy of the worksheets please email me at Dan@ThirdPowerPerformance.com.

Meal Prep

Many people don't have a lot of time during the week for cooking and don't want to eat out constantly since it is expensive and not usually healthy. One option is doing food prep. This can be a very fun family event where everyone's coming together, pitching in, and everybody kind of gets a little bit of what they want. You're creating healthy food, putting it in containers and freezing it. It's just a really nice way to bring everybody together and get on the same page for your diet.

You are increasing your health, bonding as a family, and saving money. Win-win-win!

Talk to Your Significant Other About Business Ideas

Talk to your significant other about business ideas you have while helping out with one of "their tasks." In most families, everybody has their own set of responsibilities, if you will. In my family, my wife is usually the one doing laundry. When I was working on some of these ideas, I went over while she was doing some laundry. I helped her fold things. I was talking to her about this concept, what she thinks, and tried to get her ideas on it. She gave me some good ideas that helped me flesh out what I was trying to do--being able to explain it, brought us together and helped her know what it was that I was doing. Plus, I was helping out with her task with the laundry. It was a little thing, but every little bit helps in pulling that family unit together.

It's just kind of a neat process that you're showing your significant other that you care about them. You care about their feedback, and you're willing to help them in their endeavors and the tasks that they're doing.

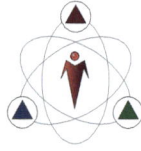

CHAPTER 8

CONCLUSION

As you can imagine this is only the tip of the iceberg.

For each of us there are a number of ways we can enhance our lives through time concentration. Think of all the activities you have in your life and how you can add more dimensions to those tasks. What pieces could you pull together? What parts can you combine? How can you pull family, friends, your health, and all the parts of life balance together into the activities that you're already doing?

That is my goal with this mini eBook. I want to get your creative juices going. Get creative. Find new and exciting ways to expand your life to make life more fulfilling. I look forward to engaging with you to help you create the life you truly want.

The full details of the Life Triad are beyond the scope of this book. Usually, my clients come for a full weekend seminar to get the core training. Several books are in the works that explain the concepts in detail. But meanwhile, I wanted to share something that can help anyone, even if they have not been through one of my programs before.

For more information about the Life Triad or our other programs, please contact us:

www.thirdpowerperformance.com

info@ThirdPowerPerformance.com

(352) 462-4518

www.facebook.com/ThirdPowerPerformance

@ThirdPowerPerf

www.linkedin.com/in/daniel-gentry

About the Author

Dan Gentry is the President of Third Power Performance, a life transformational company focused on helping high achievers maximize their potential while maintaining life balance. He takes his 30 years of experience in software and systems development, adds in 20 years in management experience in companies from small local businesses up to Fortune 10 companies, mixes in a lifetime of the study of self-improvement, and finally adds a large pinch of humor to create remarkable experiences for his audiences.

Dan is an Air Force veteran and an entrepreneur who owns several companies in the technology and insurance fields. He is the author of "99 Steps Towards Life Balance" and has another book due out this summer.

Over the past 10 years, Dan has been helping people from the Fortune 10 companies to one-person entrepreneurs to create success and Life Balance. He has helped large virtual telecommuting teams create cohesion, small company teams deal with overload and individual business owners recover their sense of purpose.

Dan is married and has five children. He lives in Central Florida with his wife and two young sons that are still at home.

www.ingramcontent.com/pod-product-compliance
Lightning Source LLC
Chambersburg PA
CBHW042107110426
42742CB00033BA/24